First World War
and Army of Occupation
War Diary
France, Belgium and Germany

30 DIVISION
Divisional Troops
149 Brigade Royal Field Artillery
27 November 1915 - 30 April 1919

WO95/2321/4

The Naval & Military Press Ltd
www.nmarchive.com
Published in association with The National Archives

Published by

The Naval & Military Press Ltd

Unit 10 Ridgewood Industrial Park,

Uckfield, East Sussex,

TN22 5QE England

Tel: +44 (0) 1825 749494

www.naval-military-press.com

www.nmarchive.com

This diary has been reprinted in facsimile from the original. Any imperfections are inevitably reproduced and the quality may fall short of modern type and cartographic standards.

© Crown Copyright
Images reproduced by permission of The National Archives, London, England, 2015.

Contents

Document type	Place/Title	Date From	Date To
Heading	WO95/2321/4 149th Bde RFA Nov 1915-Apr 1919		
Heading	30th Division Divl Artillery 149th Bde R.F.A. Nov 1915-Apr 1919		
Heading	War Diary 149th Brigade RFA 30th Division I Oct 1916-31st Oct 1916		
War Diary		02/10/1916	31/10/1916
War Diary	Guedecourt	01/10/1916	12/10/1916
War Diary	Delville Valley	15/10/1916	31/10/1916
Heading	War Diary 149th Brigade RFA 30th Division. 1st September 1916 To 30th Sept 1916		
War Diary	Festubert	01/09/1916	18/09/1916
War Diary	Hernicourt	19/09/1916	19/09/1916
War Diary	Ligny	21/09/1916	21/09/1916
War Diary	Orville	22/09/1916	22/09/1916
War Diary	Talmas	23/09/1916	23/09/1916
War Diary	Dernancourt	26/09/1916	27/09/1916
War Diary	Delville Wood	27/09/1916	30/09/1916
Heading	30th Divisional Artillery. 149th Brigade Royal Field Artillery August 1916		
War Diary	Talus-Boise (Somme)	31/07/1916	02/08/1916
War Diary	Bois-Des-Tailles (Somme)	03/08/1916	03/08/1916
War Diary	Daours	04/08/1916	05/08/1916
War Diary	Berguette Haverskerque	06/08/1916	06/08/1916
War Diary	Festubert Givenchy	10/08/1916	10/08/1916
War Diary	Locon	31/08/1916	31/08/1916
Heading	149.Bde, R.F.A. 30th Div Vol. 3		
War Diary	Suzanne	01/02/1916	25/02/1916
War Diary	Bussy	26/02/1916	28/02/1916
War Diary	Suzanne	28/02/1916	21/03/1916
War Diary	Daours	21/03/1916	24/03/1916
War Diary	Bussy-Les Daours	24/03/1916	27/03/1916
War Diary	Argoeuves	27/03/1916	05/05/1916
War Diary	Corbie	06/05/1916	06/05/1916
War Diary	Suzanne	06/05/1916	31/05/1916
War Diary	Maricourt	01/07/1916	04/07/1916
War Diary	Talus-Boise	20/07/1916	29/07/1916
Heading	30th Div Nov & Dec 15 Apr 1919		
War Diary	Larkhill	27/11/1915	28/11/1915
War Diary	Southampton	27/11/1915	28/11/1915
War Diary	Le Havre	28/11/1915	30/11/1915
War Diary	Pernois	30/11/1915	06/12/1915
War Diary	Thievres	07/12/1915	07/12/1915
War Diary	Sailly Au Bois	16/12/1915	16/12/1915
War Diary	Thievres	17/12/1915	17/12/1915
War Diary	Pernois	17/12/1915	17/12/1915
War Diary	Thievres	18/12/1915	18/12/1915
War Diary	Sailly-And-Bois	27/12/1915	27/12/1915
War Diary	Thievres	28/12/1915	28/12/1915
Heading	149th Bde. R.F.A. Vol II		

Heading	War Diary 149th (CP) Brigade R.F.A. 30th Division. From 1/1/17 To 31/1/17		
War Diary	Pernois	01/01/1917	10/01/1917
War Diary	Thalmas	10/01/1917	10/01/1917
War Diary	Pont Noyelles	11/01/1917	28/01/1917
Heading	War Diary. 149th Brigade Royal Field Artillery 1st November 1916 to 30th November 1916		
War Diary	Delville Valley	01/11/1916	21/11/1916
Heading	War Diary 149th Brigade Royal Field Artillery. 1st December 1916 To 31st December 1916		
War Diary	Lucheux	01/12/1916	03/12/1916
War Diary	Monchy Au Bois	13/12/1916	30/12/1916
War Diary	La Cauchie	01/01/1917	15/01/1917
War Diary	Lucheux	15/01/1917	31/01/1917
Heading	War Diary 149th Brigade RFA 30th Division 1st Feb 1917 To 28th Feby 1917 Vol 15		
War Diary	Mercatel Sector	02/02/1917	21/02/1917
Heading	War Diary For Month of March 1917 Of 149th (CP) Brigade R.F.A.		
War Diary	In The Line	01/03/1917	01/03/1917
War Diary	G1 Sector	04/03/1917	29/03/1917
War Diary	In The Field	01/04/1917	30/04/1917
Heading	War Diary 1-4-17 To 30-4-17 149th Bde R.F.A. 30th Division Vol 117		
Heading	War Diary 149th Brigade Royal Field Artillery 30th Division 1st To 31st May 1917		
War Diary	In The Field	03/05/1917	31/05/1917
Heading	War Diary For June 1917 149th Brigade RFA		
Heading	War Diary For June 1917 149th Brigade RFA Vol 19		
War Diary	Ypres	01/06/1917	29/06/1917
Heading	War Diary For The Month Of August 1917 149th (CP) Brigade RFA		
Heading	War Diary For The Month Of August 1917 149th (CP) Brigade RFA Vol 21		
War Diary	Zillebeke	01/08/1917	01/08/1917
War Diary	Back Arras	12/08/1917	24/08/1917
War Diary	Wytschaete	26/08/1917	31/08/1917
Heading	War Diary Vol 22 149th Bde RFA 30th Division September 1917		
War Diary	Wytschaete Area	01/09/1917	29/11/1917
War Diary	Ypres Area	01/12/1917	25/12/1917
War Diary	Ypres Sector	01/01/1918	03/01/1918
War Diary	Northern France	04/01/1918	09/01/1918
War Diary	Somme Area	10/01/1918	31/01/1918
War Diary		01/02/1918	27/02/1918
Heading	War Diary 149 Brigade R.F.A. June 1918		
War Diary		01/06/1918	30/06/1918
Heading	30th Div. War Diary Headquarters. 149th Brigade, R.F.A. March 1918		
War Diary	Savy	01/03/1918	31/03/1918
War Diary	Merville	01/04/1918	07/04/1918
War Diary	Saleux	08/04/1918	11/04/1918
War Diary	Belloy	12/04/1918	14/04/1918
War Diary	St Marie Cappel	15/04/1918	15/04/1918
War Diary	Reninghelst	16/04/1918	25/04/1918
War Diary	H 21 b 23	25/04/1918	30/04/1918

War Diary	Appendix I	21/04/1918	30/04/1918
Miscellaneous	Appendix II		
Heading	War Diary 149th. Brigade R.F.A. May 1918 Volume 31		
War Diary		05/05/1918	26/05/1918
Heading	War Diary 149th Brigade R.F.A. July 1918 Vol 32		
War Diary	Field	01/07/1918	31/07/1918
Heading	149th Brigade (County Palatine) Royal Field Artillery. War Diary August 1918		
War Diary	P II Sheet 27	01/08/1918	11/08/1918
War Diary	R 6	12/08/1918	31/08/1918
Heading	War Diary 149th Brigade R.F.A. September 1918 30th (British) Division. Vol 34		
War Diary		01/09/1918	28/09/1918
Heading	War Diary 149th Brigade R.F.A. 30th (British) Division October 1918 Vol 35		
War Diary		01/10/1918	30/10/1918
Heading	War Diary		
Heading	War Diary 149th Brigade R.F.A. 30th (British) Division. November 1918 Vol 36		
War Diary	Heestert	01/11/1918	30/11/1918
Heading	War Diary 149th Brigade, R.F.A. 30th Division. 1/31st December 1918 Vol 37		
War Diary	Aelbeke	02/12/1918	31/12/1918
Heading	War Diary of 149th Brigade, R.F.A. From 1st January 1919 To 31st January 1919		
War Diary	Aire	01/01/1919	30/04/1919

WO 95
23211 4

149th Bde RFA

Nov 1915 – Apr 1919

30TH DIVISION
DIVL ARTILLERY

149TH BDE R.F.A.
Nov ~~DEC~~ 1915 - APR 1919

30TH DIVISION
DIVL ARTILLERY

Secret.

War Diary

149th Brigade R.F.A.
30th Division.

1st Oct 1916 — 31st Oct 1916

Army Form C. 2118.

WAR DIARY
or
INTELLIGENCE SUMMARY.
(Erase heading not required.)

149 Brigade RFA 30th Division

Hour, Date, Place	Summary of Events and Information	Remarks and references to Appendices
	Changes in Officers and Casualties during Oct. 1916.	
2nd Oct 1916	2/Lt the Hon'ble G.F. Stanley admitted to Hospital	
9th Oct	Major T. Mirehouse assumed temporary Command.	
	2/Lt F.L.C. Cunningham Fairweather took on Command of R. Brigade	
15 Oct	2/Lt E. MacDonald posted to B/149 from D/150	
18 Oct	Lt W.C. Harriott D/149 Killed in action near GUEDECOURT.	
20 Oct	1 2.O.R and 24 wounded in action	
	1 O.R wounded –	
	4 O.R wounded.	
21st Oct	2/Lt B.O. Morris posted to C/149 from D.A.C.	
	2/Lt R.L. Hugh " to D.A.C from B/149	
	2/Lt G.R. Wylie A/149 wounded and admitted to hospital.	
	1 O.R wounded.	
	1 O.R Killed. 1 O.R wounded.	
24 Oct	1 O.R wounded.	
25	1 O.R Killed	
31	2/Lt J.C.P. Madden-Gaskell posted to D/149 from D.A.C	
3	Lt G.E. Jones posted to C/148 from B/149	

Major Commanding
Comdg 149 Bde RFA

WAR DIARY
or
INTELLIGENCE SUMMARY.

(Erase heading not required.)

Army Form C. 2118.

149 Brigade RFA 30 Division

Hour, Date, Place	Summary of Events and Information	Remarks and references to Appendices
3.15 pm. 10 Oct. GUEDECOURT	Co-operated with 41" D.A in operation along the line Ojectin RAINBOW TRENCH. Infy. lost the trend fearing it for fire of German dead, his flank attack being	For cancellation and change in officers see other sheet
2.12 pm 7 Oct "	Bombardment of enemy lines and infantry attack. In Brigade Zone Infantry took RAINBOW TRENCH and penetrated BACON TRENCH capturing 180 prisoners attack on flank failed & they retired from BACON TRENCH but held our consolidated RAINBOW TRENCH.	
11 Oct "	Carried out a Chinese Bombardment which from the evidence of a Captured officer etc was most successful	
12 Oct "	Tenure in general operation. In Brigade Zone our Infantry captured and held GREASE TRENCH. Attack on flanks failed.	
12 mn to 5.30pm 15 Oct DELVILLE WD	Enemy heavily shelled battery position & the Brigade zones, 5 men of aeroplanes and Rls Pillars. Destroyed gun position and also killed anga line — Casualties 12 Pillars 24 wounded.	
16 Oct	Moved A & B Batteries to a position at S.E corner of DELVILLE Wood —	
7.40. 8AM. 9.45AM. 18" Oct 18 to 31 Oct	Dispersed 3 attacks of enemy infantry against our captured trenches - Continued normal operations. All ammunition since 12 Oct has to be carried to gun positions by Pack horses. No vehicles could move.	Humphreys Rst Capt RFA Commd 149 RFA

Vol 18

SECRET

War Diary

149th Brigade R.F.A.
30th Division.

1st September 1916 to 30th Sept 1916.

Army Form C. 2118.

WAR DIARY
of
INTELLIGENCE SUMMARY.
(Erase heading not required.)

Instructions regarding War Diaries and Intelligence Summaries are contained in F. S. Regs. Part II. and the Staff Manual respectively. Title pages will be prepared in manuscript.

Place	Date	Hour	Summary of Events and Information	Remarks and references to Appendices
FESTUBERT	1.9.16		Battalion now in action covering FESTUBERT Sector.	
HERNICOURT	18.9.16 (inclusive) 19.9.16		Battalion moved to HERNICOURT Billets. Stayed one week.	
LIGNY	21.9.16		Battalion marched to LIGNY	
OEUVILLE	22.9.16		Battalion marched to OEUVILLE	
TALMAS	23.9.16		Battalion marched TALMAS stayed here 2 days	
DERNENCOURT	26.9.16		Battalion marched to DERNENCOURT	
"	26.9.16		On section of our Battery moved up to relieve section of 35th Brigade A.72. in action S. of DELVILLE WOOD	
"	27.9.16		Remainder of Battalion Relieved remainder of 35th Brigade A.72. in action N. of DELVILLE WOOD	
DELVILLE WOOD	27.9.16 & 28.9.16		In action N. of DELVILLE WOOD covering Sector L.E. of GUEUDECOURT	

[signature]
Col. Lt Colonel
[illegible]

30th Divisional Artillery.

149th BRIGADE

ROYAL FIELD ARTILLERY.

AUGUST 1916

Army Form C. 2118.

WAR DIARY
INTELLIGENCE SUMMARY.
(Erase heading not required.)

Hour, Date, Place	Summary of Events and Information	Remarks and references to Appendices
TALUS - BOISE (SOMME) 31st July / 1st Aug	The 1st Sections of Batteries relieved during the night by 276th Battery.	
" 1/2 Aug	Remaining Sections of Batteries relieved during nights joined the first Sections of Bde & remainder of Divisional Artillery at BOIS-DES-TAILLES. Major 149 FLA handed over command of Group to Major 276th Bde RFA.	
BOIS-DES-TAILLES (SOMME) 3rd Aug.	At 6.30 a.m. the whole Brigade marched via CORBIE to DAOURS	
DAOURS " 4th "	Remained at DAOURS.	
" 5th "	Brigade marched to SALEUX & entrained for BERGUETTE.	
BERGUETTE } 6th HAVERSKERQUE }	Arrived BERGUETTE detrained marched to HAVERSKERQUE, where Brigade took up billets.	
" 10th	Batteries thereupon left HAVERSKERQUE & relieved Batteries of 39th Divnl Artillery in FESTUBERT - GIVENCHY. H.Qrs	
FESTUBERT - GIVENCHY LOCON. 31st	proceeded to LOCON.	

J.G. Harbour Lieut Col for Colonel,
COMDG. 149TH (COUNTY PALATINE) BRIGADE R...

149.
Bcla.
R.F.A.
30ᵉD.ᵈ.
Vol. 3

WAR DIARY
INTELLIGENCE SUMMARY

Army Form C. 2118.

Place	Date	Hour	Summary of Events and Information	Remarks and references to Appendices
SUZANNE	1.2.16		The Brigade received orders on 21.2.16 when it was relieved by 1st LOWLAND ARTILLERY BRIGADE. Batteries had their teams up ready to retire by —	
	25.2.16		the power in their effort to leave the trenches but on 28th February a new	
BUSSY	28.2.16 to 28.2.16		day heavy fog got them in & on 28th February they moved back to BUSSY but in order to let the 118 Div A/a position on 28th the LOWLAND	
SUZANNE	29.2.16 29.2.16		Brigade having been moved over.	

G.S. Henderson and Lodd.
"a" Brigade R.F.A
Col 145

XXX Vol 4
/149 RFA

WAR DIARY
or
~~INTELLIGENCE SUMMARY~~
(Erase heading not required.)

Army Form C. 2118.

Instructions regarding War Diaries and Intelligence Summaries are contained in F.S. Regs. Part II. and the Staff Manual respectively. Title pages will be prepared in manuscript.

Place	Date	Hour	Summary of Events and Information	Remarks and references to Appendices
SUZANNE	March 1st/21st		The Brigade remained in action till 21st March, when it was relieved by the 18th Divsion. During this time, there was a fair amount of artillery activity particularly on the fronts of the two 18pdr Bys, the Brigade, particularly on the neighbourhood of KNOWLES POINT, DUCK'S POST in THE MARSH (also Quin Tunnel but before Marcelo).	
DAOURS	21st/24th March		On 20/21st the Brigade marched only line by Sailors to DAOURS, on the	
BUSSY-LES-DAOURS	24th 27th March		25th they again moved to BUSSY-LES-DAOURS and made a further move on 27th	
ARGOEUVES	27th March to 31st March		27th to ARGOEUVES, at which place the Brigade was still training at the end of the month	

A Heath
Lt Col Ca
Commdg 149 Brigade RFA

Army Form C. 2118.

149 RFA
Vol 5

WAR DIARY
or
INTELLIGENCE SUMMARY.

(Erase heading not required.)

Place	Date	Hour	Summary of Events and Information	Remarks and references to Appendices
ARGOEUVES	April 1917 Apr 30		The Brigade remained in training at ARGOEUVES during the whole of the month.	

G K Smyth
Lieut Colonel,
Commanding 149th Brigade RFA.

HQ 149 RFA Bde Aug 6 XXX

Army Form C. 2118.

WAR DIARY
INTELLIGENCE SUMMARY.
(Erase heading not required.)

Place	Date	Hour	Summary of Events and Information	Remarks and references to Appendices
ARQUEVES	5/5/16 to 5.8.16		Brigade still in rest billets & training. Marched to CORBIE on 5.5.16	
CORBIE	6.5.16		Brigade marched to take action N.E. of SUZANNE	
SUZANNE	6.5.16 to 10.5.16		Brigade took over action in various places. Cpl. R. Ross at on 13th Bingo. Enemy attempts a raid on trenches manned by Brigade, which was repulsed. G.O.C. Reports have been complimentary remarks about work of Batteries during the Raid.	

J Stanley Montagu
-Brigade O.C.
6 Aug 1943

June

Army Form C. 2118.

149 RFA
Vol Y

WAR DIARY
INTELLIGENCE SUMMARY.
(Erase heading not required.)

Hour, Date, Place	Summary of Events and Information	Remarks and references to Appendices
SUZANNE.	The Brigade was in action from the position near SUZANNE and a howitzer position S.of MARICOURT preparatory to the attack on the enemy's lines. Preliminary bombardment started on 24.6.16. The history of the Brigade was roughly as follows: for five days C.B. work on a front of 6000 yards firing 200 rounds per gun per day. C.B. the ½ of the 1st day. He Infantry advanced & the Brigade fired a barrage in front of them and 2.5 hours after the attack. The Brigade helped to catch the Infantry on the 2nd & 3rd days in consolidating the ground by firing barrages on all known counter-attack avenues, also catching prisoners & clearing the enemy's second & third lines & clearing reserve lines. On Infantry being withdrawn, the Brigade kept pushing into the battle, the services being used very accurate.	Signed Hughes M... Col. N.5th Division R.F.A.

WAR DIARY or INTELLIGENCE SUMMARY

Army Form C. 2118.

30.

149 R.F.A.

Place	Date	Hour	Summary of Events and Information	Remarks and references to Appendices
MARICOURT	1.7.16		On 1st July 1916 the attack on Montauban took place. The Brigade cooperating. The attack was successful chiefly owing to the very thorough Artillery preparation. The Gunners Subr' Corps (20th (Dvndl)) were on our right, the 18th Division on our left. Both objectives were captured immediately, namely DUBLIN TRENCH & GLATZ REDOUBT by the 89th Infy Bde & 21st Infantry Brigades respectively, also MONTAUBAN by the 90th Infy Bde. Later the 89th Infy Bde captured the BRIQUETERIE, all artillery preparation support during these operations took part in by the Brigade arty.	
"	3.7.16 4.7.16		The Brigade Arty supported the 89th Infy Bde & Captain BERNAFAY WOOD on the 3rd and Rights of all Battns of the Bde attained to Trigonometric North West of MARICOURT. During the following work, the Brigade cooperated with the Infantry during various attacks which culminated in the complete capture of TRONE'S WOOD & the establishment of a line immediately WEST of MALTZ HORN FARM. After this operation the Brigade cooperated supported the Infantry of 18th Division who relieved the Infantry of the 30th Divn.	
TALUS - BOISE	20.7.16 - 21.7.16		Later the cooperation was with the Infantry of the 35th Division ie the 30 Mc Brigade from the relief the C.R.A. 35th Divn & on the 21st July B HQ moved to the TALUS BOISE in liaison with the Infantry of 35th Division, Batteries remaining in the same position. During the following days cooperated in minor operations which included preparation on the GERMAN Trenches on MALTZ HORN FARM RIDGE and on GUILLEMONT-FALFEMONT FARM front. & much on the an excellent preparation on the Artillery. All this time every F.K. assistance expenditure. I command the the Brigade higher to observe any wear whatever manner was necessary for the Brigade to ascertain that opportunity fire which was awaited for the operation in hand.	
	29.7.16		On the 29th July, artillery preparation commenced for the attack on the GUILLEMONT-FALFEMONT FARM line, Brigades by the 35th Division 18., 89th to 90th Infantry have been brought back into the line for this purpose. The Brigade made indirect support of the self contents which were made by the 90th Infy Bde. The attacks were in cooperation with the French Infantry on our Right by the Rifle Division on our left. Figure it will be seen the Brigade was in action during the operations without the presentation for the 1st June the from the 30th Division on the GUILLEMONT- FALFEMONT FARM LINE. The endurance of the men during these many trying conditions was remarkable ***	

Signed: [signature]
OC 149 Bde R.F.A.

149 & I. Bde: 27a.
Vol: I

131/7936

30/4/49

Nos rbec 15
Apr '49

Army Form C. 2118

WAR DIARY
INTELLIGENCE SUMMARY.
(Erase heading not required.)

Instructions regarding War Diaries and Intelligence Summaries are contained in F. S. Regs., Part II and the Staff Manual respectively. Title pages will be prepared in manuscript.

Place	Date	Hour	Summary of Events and Information	Remarks and references to Appendices
LARKHILL	27.11.15		Entrained for SOUTHAMPTON DOCKS	
	28.11.15			
SOUTHAMPTON	27.11.15		Embarked for FRANCE	
	28.11.15			
LE HAVRE	28.11.15		Disembarked	
	29.11.15			
"	29.11.15		Entrained for DOULLENS	
	30.11.15			
PERNOIS	30.11.15		Arrived & went into billets.	
"	1.12.15			
	6.12.15		A & B Batteries marched to THIEVRES	
THIEVRES	7.12.15		A & B Batteries marched to SAILLY-au-BOIS to go into action, attached to 48th Division	
SAILLY au BOIS	16.12.15		A & B Batteries marched to THIEVRES	
THIEVRES	17.12.15		A & B Batteries returned to PERNOIS	
PERNOIS	17.12.15		C & D Batteries marched to THIEVRES	
THIEVRES	18.12.15		C & D Batteries marched to SAILLY-au-BOIS to go into action, attached to 48th Division	
SAILLY au BOIS	27.12.15		C & D Batteries marched to THIEVRES	
THIEVRES	28.12.15		C & D Batteries returned to PERNOIS	

149 Bell: R-7a.
Vol: II

Secret.

Vol/4

War Diary
149th (9) Brigade R.F.A
30th Division

From 1/1/17
To 31/1/17

Army Form C. 2118.

WAR DIARY
or
INTELLIGENCE SUMMARY.
(Erase heading not required.)

Instructions regarding War Diaries and Intelligence Summaries are contained in F. S. Regs., Part II. and the Staff Manual respectively. Title pages will be prepared in manuscript.

Place	Date	Hour	Summary of Events and Information	Remarks and references to Appendices
PERNOIS	1st/10			
THALMAS	10th			
PONT NOYELLES	11th			
	12th		No action NORTH of SUZANNE.	
	28th		The Brigade took part in the defence of BRAY when attacked by the Germans.	
			has been heavily shelled all day with her usual shells.	

2353 Wt. W3544/1454 700,000 5/15 D. D. & L.   A.D.S.S./Forms/C. 2118.

SECRET

WAR DIARY.

149th Brigade Royal Field Artillery.

1st November 1916   to   30th November 1916.

Army Form C. 2118.

WAR DIARY
or
INTELLIGENCE SUMMARY.
(Erase heading not required.)

149 Brigade RFA   November 1916   30 November

Place	Date	Hour	Summary of Events and Information	Remarks and references to Appendices
DELVILLE Valley	1st Nov		Grenier Bombardment 2 other Ranks killed.	
	2nd		Lieut a/c J.S. Holder slightly wounded	
	3rd Nov	6am	Cooperated with Chinese Bombardment on R.n.R of 2nd Australian Div dummy attack on HILT Trench	
	6 Nov	2 pm	Bombardment of STORMY Trench during Chinese Bombardment in connection with 2nd Corps Div Arty.	
	8 Nov		2nd Lieut E MARCHETTI killed at gun position D/149. 5 other Ranks wounded.	
	9/10 Nov	2 am	Chinese Bombardment	
	12 Nov		Lieut E. MACDONALD slightly wounded —	
	13 Nov		1 other Rank wounded	
	14 Nov	5.45am	Chinese Bombardment on whole IV Army front to arouse attack on 10 unsuccessful.	
	16 Nov		1 other R.n.R wounded.	
	17		1 other R.n.R wounded	
	18		Relieved by 21st Brigade RA attaching gun unicas Brimmer at MERLANCOURT the night. The whole unit was chiefly employed for been ment and antenna condition of consultation during operation from 27 Sept — 18 Nov. Killed 2 Lieuts HESHETH and MARCHETTI 2nd Lieut WYLLIE — Lieut & lieut HATTON Lieut E. MACDONALD — other Ranks killed 16	
			Wounded 37	
			March to BONNAY	
19			" TALMAS	
20			" LUCHEUX	
21			AT LUCHEUX till end of month.	

Humpton Kennethinde
Capt 149 15th RFA.

SECRET.

WAR DIARY.

149th Brigade Royal Field Artillery.

1st December 1916 to 31st December 1916.

Army Form C. 2118.

WAR DIARY
or
INTELLIGENCE SUMMARY.
(Erase heading not required.)

149 Brigade R.F.A. 30th Division

Hour, Date, Place	Summary of Events and Information	Remarks and references to Appendices
1st & 2nd Dec LUCHEUX	In rest billets	
3rd	Brigade marched to LA CAUCHIE and relieved 232 Brigade 46 Division in the MONCHY AU BOIS section of the line.	
13th Dec MONCHY AU BOIS	Bombarded enemy front line during the day and supported an Infantry raid by 89 Inf. Brigade during the night.	
23rd	Bombarded enemy front line trenches in accordance with 30 Div A.5.04 order.	
30th	Co-operated with 46th Div. Arty in bombardment of Essarts B.1.	
	Casualties during month 1 O.R. wounded	

Newman H.K. Lt Col
Comdg 149 Bde RFA
2/1/917

WAR DIARY
or
INTELLIGENCE SUMMARY

Army Form C. 2118.

149 Bde. R.F.A.
30 & Division

Place	Date	Hour	Summary of Events and Information	Remarks and references to Appendices
La CAUCHIE			MONCHY-au-BOIS Front	
	1/1/17 – 14/1/17		Nothing to report	
	15/1/17		Casual and Bombardment of Enemy Communication Trenches & Batteries	
			Co-operated with RFA Group & with Group in Bombardment of Enemy O.T's & Strong points	
	29/1/17		One Battalion per day relieved by Batteries of 245 Bde. R.F.A. 149 & F.A	
	—		Remnants of Bde. relieved	
LUCHEUX	15/1/17		Bde. Billeted in LUCHEUX for training etc.	
	30/1/17		Three inspections by Bridge in marching order by G.O.R.A., C.O. 30 Div. & General Uffery	
	31/1/17		One section of E/149 came to 3/149 to make the Bty. up to 6 Hors Btys.	
	31/1/17		Bde. marched to MONCHIET	
			Travelling during month nil	
			Weather very cold 3-4 inches of snow and severe frost during the whole of the month.	

J.G. Hackworth Lt Col R.F.A
for O/c 149 Bde. R.F.A.

SECRET Vol 15

War Diary.

149th Brigade R.F.A.
30th Division

1st Feby 1917 to 28th Feby 1917

Army Form C. 2118.

WAR DIARY
or
INTELLIGENCE SUMMARY.
(Erase heading not required.)

149 Brigade RFA 30th Division

Hour, Date, Place	Summary of Events and Information	Remarks and references to Appendices
February 1917 MERCATEL Sector	Brigade engaged in preparing forward position - No operations - front very quiet -	
2nd Feb	2nd Lieut A.H. OXLEY B/149 Slightly wounded	
16th Feb	2nd Lieut W.S. HILL joined + posted to C/149 -	
10th Feb	2nd Lieut J.C. CURRIE C/149 apprentice to RFA 2nd Cav Div.	
20 Feb	2 O R C/149 wounded -	
21st Feb	2nd Lieut P. HENNAN D/149 transferred to W.30. T.M	

Maynard H.M.
Capt 149 B/RFA

SECRET.

War Diary for Month of March 1917 Vol 16

of

149th (C.P.) Brigade R.F.A.

WAR DIARY or INTELLIGENCE SUMMARY

Army Form C. 2118.

149 Brigade RFA

Hour, Date, Place	Summary of Events and Information	Remarks and references to Appendices
1st March – In the line G.1 Section	Capt. LUXMORE left on attachment to III Corps R.A. 1 O.R. wounded – C/149	
4th	Major IMBERT TERRY B/149 struck off strength sick in England –	
7	2nd Lt JEMMETT (6ft 9½") posted A/149. 2nd Lt R.A. STEWART posted B/149 –	
9	2nd Lt BROSTER posted A/149	
15		
18	Corporation in successful raid on enemy trenches –	
4 am	Infantry reported enemy evacuating his Front line system. Batteries ordered to support position on CRINCHON River and regalia	
[?] 1 pm	Foos followed Infantry. H.Q.P. moved to dug-out in AGNY Sunken Road	
20th	Brigade advanced at dawn and occupied position near Railway 1500 yards East of former Enemy Front Line, relieved by 2nd Lt MOORE who has done very good work following the Infantry and keeping up communication.	
22nd	Anger Bros moved to BLAIREVILLE	
23rd	Wagn Lin limber on of BLAIREVILLE	
25th	Capt MACFARLANE arrived and posted as adjt MAJOR to B/149	
26·27·28·29·30·31st	Engaged all night in carrying amm. up to forward position selected for offensive against HINDENBURG Line – 1 Sergt D/149 wounded.	
29th	Major J.H. NUNN A/149 fatally wounded when near our front line.	

[signed] H. [?]
Comdg 149 Bde RFA

Army Form C. 2118.

WAR DIARY
INTELLIGENCE SUMMARY.
(Erase heading not required.)

Instructions regarding War Diaries and Intelligence Summaries are contained in F. S. Regs. Part II and the Staff Manual respectively. Title pages will be prepared in manuscript.

Place	Date	Hour	Summary of Events and Information	Remarks and references to Appendices
In the field.	1.4.17.		The month opened with very bad weather and snow fell heavily. The Brigade was in action near Railway in M.27 with H.Q at AGNY.	
	2nd.		HENIN Captured.	
	3rd		Though weather was still very bad & snow on the ground the Brigade moved to position from which to take on the COJEUL SWITCH at a range of about 5000 yards.	
	4th		Bombardment of HINDENBURG LINE.	
	5th		" " " "	
	6th		" " " "	
	7th		" " " "	
	8th		" " " " 89th Infantry Brigade supported by 149th & 148th Brigades R.F.A. and 150th Army F.A. Bde captured ST.MARTIN.	
	9th		General advance commenced. 21st Inft Bde met considerable difficulty E of NEUVILLE VITASSE by M.G fire; but succeeded in getting in when assisted by troops from North. 89th I. Bde failed. 2/Lieut Walker & 2/Lieut Musson did good work in rendering reports of the situation.	
	10th		Attack renewed on line N. of COJEUL River. Considerable number of prisoners taken. Teams were standing by for Brigade advance but this was not able to be done.	
	11th		Situation quiet.	
	12th		HENINEL captured & Cavalry seen E of MONCHY le PREUX.	
	13th		Bde advanced. Batteries to new positions S of COJEUL River, H.Q to Rly cutting T.20 central, all in action by 6am. Fine morning and satisfactory registration carried out.	

WAR DIARY
INTELLIGENCE SUMMARY.
(Erase heading not required.)

Army Form C. 2118.

Instructions regarding War Diaries and Intelligence Summaries are contained in F. S. Regs., Part II. and the Staff Manual respectively. Title pages will be prepared in manuscript.

Place	Date	Hour	Summary of Events and Information	Remarks and references to Appendices
	15th		Came under Command of the 21st Division. Back areas kept under fire.	
	16th		Quiet.	
	17th		The Brigade was in liasion with the 100th Inf. Bde.	
	18-19th		Quiet. Move by Batteries impending.	
	20th		Capture of CHERISY.	
	21st		Batteries moved to T.3.b with H.Q 2000yds in rear.	
	23rd		Attack by 50th & 33rd Divisions failed, but during night enemy retired and objectives were occupied.	
	26th		18pdr Batteries moved to new position in T.10.b.	
	30th		Came under 18th Divnl Arty.	

Lieut R.F.A & Adjutant.,
for O.C., 149th Brigade Royal Field Artillery.

149 Bde R.F.A

War 1917 Diary 1-4-17 to 30-4-17

30th Division

149 Bde R⁄A 30
Ap 17

Secret

SECRET.

Vol 18

WAR DIARY.

149th BRIGADE ROYAL FIELD ARTILLERY.   **30th DIVISION.**

1st to 31st MAY 1917.

Army Form C. 2118.

WAR DIARY
or
INTELLIGENCE SUMMARY.
(Erase heading not required.)

Instructions regarding War Diaries and Intelligence Summaries are contained in F. S. Regs., Part II. and the Staff Manual respectively. Title pages will be prepared in manuscript.

Place	Date	Hour	Summary of Events and Information	Remarks and references to Appendices
In the field.	3rd May 1917.		3rd May. 149th Bde R.F.A took part(with 18th Divnl Infantry) in attack on FONTAINE & CHERISY, in conjunction with 5th Army attack on BULLECOURT. Infantry obtained objectives in parts, but by evening were back on their original lines after enemy counter attacks. Bombardment in evening to allow lost Companies to be brought back. This was accomplished. Brigade fired 650rds 18pdr & 1500 Rds 4.5 How during day. 2/Lieut V.J.Gallie as Brigade F.O.O. for 36 hours. Proved impossible to keep line to Battalion H.Q going.	
	10th.		"D" Battery withdrawn from line to Wagon Lines.	
	11th.		Change of Brigade Zone, involving change of O.P's.	
	8-12th.		Shelling about Battery Positions in T.10.b. increased. 1 gun "C" Battery knocked out.	
	13th.		New positions in T.16.c reconnoitred and occupied by A & B Batteries.	
	20th.		Brigade co-operated in attack on HINDENBURG line by 33rd Division on right. Attack successful. Especially successful shooting by batteries on enemy advancing to counter attack helped to secure this.	
	21st.		Brigade withdrew to Wagon Lines preparatory to leaving the area.	
	23rd.		Brigade marched to HABARCQ via FICHEUX and WAILLY.	
	24th.		March continued to MAISNIL St POL(3 miles from water !)	
	25th.		Bde marched again via St POL and PERNES to AMETTES, longest days march, 18 miles and very hot.	

Army Form C. 2118.

WAR DIARY
or
INTELLIGENCE SUMMARY.
(Erase heading not required.)

Instructions regarding War Diaries and Intelligence Summaries are contained in F.S. Regs., Part II. and the Staff Manual respectively. Title pages will be prepared in manuscript.

Place	Date	Hour	Summary of Events and Information	Remarks and references to Appendices
In the field	26th May.		March continued Wm.AIRE to WITTES, staying there on 29th.	
	28th.		Brigade moved on to BORRE via HAZEBROUCK. Battery Commanders went on to YPRES to see new positions.	
	29th.		Brigade marched to WATOU area.	
	30th.		End of march in reaching Wagon lines just S.E of POPERINGHE. 1 Section per Battery moved into the line at night.	
	31st.		Bde H.Q. & remaining 2 Sections of Batteries moved up into the line & took over, covering the 80th Infantry Brigade.	
			Casualties during month of May:- Lieut J.D.Newsom & 2/Lieut V.J.Gallie Wounded slightly remaining at duty. 9 Other Ranks wounded, 4 wounded slightly remaining at duty.	

[signature]

Lieut-Colonel R.F.A.,
Commanding 149th Brigade R.F.A.

Mac Leary
for
JUNE
1917

149th Brigade R.F.A.

War Diary
for
JUNE 1917.
149th Brigade R.F.A.

Army Form C. 2118.

WAR DIARY
INTELLIGENCE SUMMARY

149 Brigade RFA 30th Div.

(Erase heading not required.)

Place	Date	Hour	Summary of Events and Information	Remarks and references to Appendices
YPRES	1st June		Brigade became responsible for covering the left of the line late by 89th Infantry Brigade	Reference Map Lens 1/40 Sheet 7a
	2nd		2/Lt NEWSOM and GALLIE slightly wounded -	
	3		Battalion heavily shelled in position on YPRES Mont -	
	4		Heavy shelling by day and very heavy gas shelling at night	
	5th		Counter raid by 89th Inf Bde, very satisfactory - 1 Prisoner - 2 slight casualties	
	6th		Par up four bombardments along 30 Div front.	
	7th		Shelling continued - Expended with barrages and fugitive shelling T	
			Relief attack on WYTSCHAETE - MESSINES Ridge -	
			General communication and CLONMEL Copse - Fruitful diversion counter attack against left of our immediate	
			Battalion front all day - 2nd Lt JOHNSON A/149 Killed - 4 O.R wounded (2 since of wounds)	
	8th		A/149 severely shelled 1 Gun destroyed 1.O.R wounded	
	9th		Heavy shelling by day and ar night - into gun pits - B/149 one gun damaged by hostile fire	
	13th		Counter raid by 90th Inf Bde - very successful - Bombardment forward positions	
	14		D/149 heavy shelled 1 How destroyed 3.O.R wounded -	
	16		Battalion moved to position at HELLBLAST Corner. 2 section per battery	
	17		Remaining section + B.M H.Q move to forward position - D/149 heavily shelled 2 Hows destroyed	
	18		Enemy Air Craft very active	
	19		D/149 heavily shelled Major Hubbard DSO wounded	
	20		Batt in action on Battery position	
	21		do	
			5 O.R wounded	
	23		Hostile Arty very active all day and at night own gun shells	
	24		" " " C/149 two guns damaged by hostile fire	
	25th		" " " 4 " "	
	29		Moved out to rest or change lines. Killed 1 Officer - 7.O.R. Wounded -	
			Total Casualties for month Killed 4	
			Killed	Officer - OR -
			Wounded at duty	3	34
			Remaining at duty	4	11
			Total Casualties 64	

Mrs Lacey
for the hands
of August 1917

149 # (OF) Brigade RFA

Vol 21

War Diary
for August 1917
of
114th (H) Brigade R.F.A.
(CD)

Confidential

WAR DIARY
or
INTELLIGENCE SUMMARY.
(Erase heading not required.)

Army Form C. 2118.

August 1917.

Place	Date	Hour	Summary of Events and Information	Remarks and references to Appendices
ZILLEBEKE	1/8/17		Having taken part in the attacks of July 31st the Bde remained in action defending the line until Aug 10th when they pulled out to Wagon Lines near OUDERDOM	
	12th		Bde left OUDERDOM and marched to BAILLEUL	
Back Areas	14th		Left BAILLEUL and marched to STEENWERK	5 BFA
	16th		Left STEENWERK and marched to STRAZEELE	
	24th		Bde rested for 7 days relieving the 4th Aust Bde in the line near WYTSCHAETE	3 BFA
WYTSCHAETE	26/27		Bde took part in barrage for Raid by the 112th Inf Bde on BEE Farm	
	3/1		Bde took part in barrage for Raid by the 111th Inf Bde on SPIDER Hge	

Casualties. Officers O.Rs.
K W Gassed   K   W   Gassed
1   3   35   3

Total Casualties while in the YPRES SALIENT

OFFICERS
KILLED WOUNDED GASSED
3   11   3
about 50%

O.Rs.
KILLED WOUNDED GASSED
38   115   27
TOTAL 194. about 25%

Adjutant 149th Brigade R.F.A.

Secret

War Diary

Vol 22

149th Bde R.F.A.

30th Division

September 1917

Army Form C. 2118.

WAR DIARY
INTELLIGENCE SUMMARY.
(Erase heading not required.)

SEPTEMBER 1917.

Place	Date	Hour	Summary of Events and Information	Remarks and references to Appendices
WYTSCHAETE AREA.	Oct 1 to 13		The Bde was in action in the WYTSCHAETE Area defending the line held by 30 Divl Infantry.	
	14.			
	15. to 20		The Bde took part in Army + Corps practice barrages and carried out extensive harassing fire by night on tracks etc behind enemy front line.	
	to 26		This was continued after the attack on the 20th up to the 26th when the renewed attack took place. The Division automatically passed out of the IX Corps into the VIII Corps on a rearrangement of Corps frontsYPRES-COMINES	
	27th		Bde advised of extension of Divl front up to the Canal, and the departure of the 49th D. Arty leaving the 104th + 145th 74.9 Bdes to defend the front. C. Battery moved to occupy a position vacated by the 49th Dir arty, so as to be better able to defend the northern part of the front.	
	28th			
	29th to 30		The front remained fairly quiet but hostile Aircraft made use of many of hostile bombing attacks on our Support Areas. —	
			Casualties 2 O.R wounded by H.A. fire.	
			2 O.R " by H Aircraft Bombs.	

for O.C 149 Bde R.F.A.
Capt + adjt

Army Form C. 2118.

149 th R.F.A.

Vol 23

WAR DIARY
or
INTELLIGENCE SUMMARY.
(Erase heading not required.)

OCTOBER

Place	Date	Hour	Summary of Events and Information	Remarks and references to Appendices
WYTSCHAETE & KEMMEL Area				
	Oct 4		C/149 took part in attack by putting up a Smoke Screen on the Western Slopes of the ZANDVOORDE Ridge.	
	1–31		Silent Periods were observed conforming with the attacks further North.	
			Visual Signalling successfully put into operation from all Bde O.Ps.	
			Battery positions greatly improved + considerable work done preparing for the Winter.	
			C Batty were unfortunate in having 3 men killed by one 77/A shell and one man by anti aircraft shell.	
			Casualties. 1 Officer – hospital sick.	
			4 OR Killed.	
			2 OR Wounded.	

F. Bowman
Capt. + adjt
for OC 149 Bde R.F.A.

149 Bde RFA
Army Form C. 2118.

WAR DIARY
or
INTELLIGENCE SUMMARY.
(Erase heading not required.)

November 1917. Vol 24

Place	Date	Hour	Summary of Events and Information	Remarks and references to Appendices
WYTSCHAETE	Nov 1st to		The Bde continued in Action in the WYTSCHAETE Area, where the general conditions remained quiet.	CASUALTIES
	6th		Lieut R H PEAKE was appointed Bde signalling officer & there were leave amongst drivers by A. A. gunfire.	
	9th		Capt D E JONES left the Bde to command a Batty in the 33rd Div Arty.	
	10th		Attack day further North resulted in heavy firing from enemy Arty located in the area of Comines.	
	12th		Batteries moved at 10 am to their Wagon lines the front being taken over by the 148 Bde + 189 Bde.	
			The pers of B. + D were left in position. 13th Advanced parties went to METEREN.	
	14th		Lieut MOORE promoted Captain to D Batty. Bde marched to METEREN.	
	15th		Lieut GOZZIE " Captain A Batty. Bde remained at METEREN until 18th inst	
	18th		Gun X° for Batty moved into Action S.E. of YPRES in SANCTUARY WOOD.	
	19th		Remainder of Bde moved to Action = HQ moved to TUILLERIES. + Col thereon commanded.	
	24th		148 + 149 Bdes an Northern group. 24th Col MASTERS left for Leave. Col W JEEP DSO returned + commanded with 149 Bde. Bde Staff until the 28th when his own (148) staff relieved.	
	28th		Practice Barrage for the Capture of POLDERHOEK CHATEAU carried out	
	29th		Lieut ESSEY + HINWELL joined Bde + joined A + C Batteries respectively.	

K.... air-raid
L.OC/149 RFA

WAR DIARY
or
INTELLIGENCE SUMMARY.
Army Form C. 2118.

149 B*de* R.F.A

Vol 25

DECEMBER 1917

Place	Date	Hour	Summary of Events and Information	Remarks and references to Appendices
YPRES AREA	Tue 1		The Batteries of the Brigade remained in action covering the POLDERHOEK Sector. (The Bde H.Q were out of action) together with the Batteries of the 148 Bde, & were commanded by Lt Col Jelf D.S.O as Northern Group.	
	Dec 16		The 149 Bde H.Q relieved Lt Col Jelf D.S.O. & the Northern Group was commanded by Lt Col Trotters. The Enemy shewed no marked activity until Dec 23rd when he used Gas shells in the vicinity of Batteries and two men of C/149 became casualties. Reserve positions were chosen for A & C Batteries to enable them to defend the Corps Line, & work was commenced, though Snow & Frost further delayed progress.	
	Dec 27		HQ Staff was relieved by the 148 Bde. Batteries remained in action.	
	Dec 25		All Batteries arranged very successful Xmas dinners, Pork & Beer being the Fare & the Gunners in action were relieved so as to have their Xmas dinner on New Years Day.	M Cowan Capt & adjt for OC 149 Bde R.F.A

Army Form C. 2118.

149 Bde R.F.A
Vol 26

WAR DIARY
INTELLIGENCE SUMMARY
(Erase heading not required)

Place	Date	Hour	Summary of Events and Information	Remarks and references to Appendices
YPRES SECTOR	June 1918 1st		Battalion in action. Bde Hq at RENINGHELST.	
"	2nd		2/Lt Kame Wayport & Jay hr attached from 30"Bde.	
"	3rd		Capt W.H. BLOOR killed in action. 2/Lt C/Morgan attached from 30 Bde. Severely wounded.	
NORTHERN FRANCE	4th		Brigade marched to FLETRE.	
"	5th		" " MORBECQUE.	
"	6th		" " RENESCURE.	
"	8th		" " MORBECQUE area to entrain at 3am 9th.	
"	9th		Train accident at STEENBECQUE. Entrained to THENNES to entrain. Bde HQ entrained at STEENBECQUE 10pm 9th. marched off 11am 10th.	
SOMME AREA	10th		Detrained LONGEAU 11am 10th marched to DOMART.	
"	11th		Bde remained at DOMART.	
"	12th		Brigade marched to QUESNEL. (about 7 miles)	
"	13th		" " ROIGLISE (" 12 ")	
"	27th		" " VOYENNES	
"	31st		Remained at VOYENNES.	

3/6

[Signed] Captain R.H.A.
p.o.c. 149 Bde R.F.A.

WAR DIARY
or
INTELLIGENCE SUMMARY.

Place	Date	Hour	Summary of Events and Information	Remarks and references to Appendices
	1st		Brigade at VOYENNES: training	
	16th			
	19th		1 Section of D Battery moved into action : C Battery under 61st Division	
	20th		Remaining 2 sections of Battery of Brigade went into action	
	21st		Bde HQ went into action at SAVY but did not function until 23rd	
	24th		CRA and BM inspects Anti-Tank guns and positions	
	27th		D Battery moved two guns back to alternative position	

SECRET

War Diary.

149 Brigade R.F.A

June 1918.

Army Form C. 2118.

WAR DIARY
or
INTELLIGENCE SUMMARY.
(Erase heading not required.)

Place	Date	Hour	Summary of Events and Information	Remarks and references to Appendices
	1st June		Brigade out of the line : rest & training in RACQUINGHEM Area Morning	
	(6th)		Allier proceeded to 2nd Army Artillery School (TILQUES) as Instructional Battery	
	(2nd)		Divisional Artillery festival Exercise carried out. (Horse Recreates & also up : an advance guard)	
	7th		Brigade placed in G.H.Q. reserve	
	15		Brigade moved up to SERCUS area	
	17th		Brigade (less Allier) went into action with 29th D.A. position in & about Fort de Nieppe. Gun O.P. wounded in occupying position.	
	20th		Brigade withdrew to camps at VERCUS area	
	25th		Left (Sqndrn (Maj A.Bell)) moved into action on Fr Arre near MOREUVRE 28/3/48 to 4/4/18	
	26th		Brigade (less A Bty) moved into action to support 28th S.A. (moving 31st div) in operation Gave Marse S	
	28th		Barrage fired to cover operation of 31st Div Operation completely successful	
	29th		Counter preparation S.O.S. (John Marie) fires. Dry Marine front	
	30th	3.60	First fired as for 20 minute. No change in schedule. Day quiet tabs. Fine weather	

R. Blunden Major R.F.A
Col. 149 Bde R.F.A
for D.C 149 Bde R.F.A.

30th Div.

WAR DIARY

Headquarters,

149th BRIGADE, R.F.A.

M A R C H

1 9 1 8

30 Div
149. Bde. R.F.A.
Army Form C. 2118.

WAR DIARY
or
INTELLIGENCE SUMMARY
(Erase heading not required.)

MARCH 1918.   VII 28

Place	Date	Hour	Summary of Events and Information	Remarks and references to Appendices
SAVY.	1/3/18.		The Bde was in action covering the ST QUENTIN front with Bde H.Q at VAUX, and wagon lines at GERMAINE. Considerable amount of work was done on positions for the defence of Battle lines and ammunition up to 200 rds per gun was dumped in readiness.	
"	2/3/18.		At about 4:30 a.m. the enemy attacked and [launching] MANCHESTER REDOUBT approached our positions near SAVY from the South. Troops were in readiness but far off, but A/149 had to abandon their guns (thin in all) and D/149 lost 2 teams of a forward section and also on tour which had been run forward about 500x. They managed to get the remaining three away. B/149 retired with all guns intact to Battle positions. 22/3/18 C/149 retired from No 4 HOLNON WOOD complete.	
	22/3/18.		The battle was extremely hard from battle positions until about 3 p.m. when our Infantry informed us they could hold out no longer, the Batteries took up position near FORTH fired about 1 wagon per gun & then retired under orders to FOLANCOURT W of HAM.	
	23/3/18.		Positions were occupied at dawn to defend HAM, but were forced to retire to vicinity of ESMERY-HALLON about 10 a.m. Great exhaustion was obtained.	

WAR DIARY or INTELLIGENCE SUMMARY

Army Form C. 2118.

Place	Date	Hour	Summary of Events and Information	Remarks and references to Appendices
	23/3/18		and heavy casualties inflicted on the enemy.	
	24/3/18		24th/3/18. 4 pm the positions E of ERCHEU, where again good shooting was down on the enemy as they descended the slopes from ESMERY HALLON. At night the Batteries moved to depot at LANNOY Bridge. Very heavy fire was kept up most of the day, but South wing had to retire at dusk about 2000x to SOLENTIE and at about 9 pm Bde was ordered to return to ROISPISE. The enemy having entered ERCHEU.	
	25/3/18		25/3/18. After 2 hours rest positions was occupied, but after only a little shooting Bde had to retire to position just E of BEAUVRAINS — good observations found about 1000yds in front with good effect before the French Infantry Division on our left withdrew & Bde had to withdraw to MESNIL ST GEORGE via FAVEROLLE & MONTDIDIER.	
	27/3/18		27/3/18. The CO Bde ordered to underground at DAVENESCOURT but Bosch captured the villages about Noon. Batteries were diverted & put in Action near PLESSIER at night.	
	28/3/18		28/3/18. Bde retired to positions between PLESSIER & MIREVIL about midday and again about 4 pm retired to positions just E of MAILLY when the Enemy captured PLESSIER.	
	29/3/18		29/3/18. Good shooting on enemy entering MOREVIL, but when BRACHES was captured about 7 pm, Batteries were forced to retire to positions E of NERVILLE	
	30/31		Batteries remained in action & held up the enemy.	

for O.C.
Capt & adjt
149 Bde RFA

149 Brigade R.F.A. 30

Army Form C. 2118.

WAR DIARY
or
INTELLIGENCE SUMMARY.
(Erase heading not required.)

Vol 29 APRIL 1918

Place	Date	Hour	Summary of Events and Information	Remarks and references to Appendices
MERVILLE	1/4/18		Batteries remained in action in positions just E. of MERVILLE covering the French holding the MERVILLE – MAILLY-RAINEVAL Sector. Bde H.Q. was in MERVILLE.	
	2/4/18		The Brigade was relieved at dawn by the 148 Bde. Batteries withdrew to their respective wagon lines in JUMEL.	
	3/4/18		Brigade resting in JUMEL.	
	4/4/18	5.15 pm	Brigade was ordered to come into action West of JUMEL to cover the line ROUVREL – MERVILLE. Bde H.Q. moved to Farm on JUMEL-ESSERTAUX ROAD	
	5/4/18	2 pm	Brigade received orders to prepare to advance – Positions were reconnoitred occupied just N. of AILLY-SUR-NOYE to assist in French counter attack at 4.30 pm. The Enemy retired in am of BOIS de L'ARRIERE COUR & attack did not therefore take place.	
	6/4/18		All Batteries registered from a Brigade O.P. established at MON IDÉE Farm – a great deal of harassing fire was carried out, especially in the evening 6/7 final. Received a warning order for withdrawal of Brigade	
	7/4/18		Advance billetting party left JUMEL at 2.30 pm for SALEUX (S. of AMIENS). At the request of the French, concentration shoots were fired during the day. The Brigade withdrew from the line at 8 pm & marched to rest billets in SALEUX	

149 Bde R.F.A. Army Form C. 2118.

APRIL 1918 Sheet II

WAR DIARY
or
INTELLIGENCE SUMMARY.
(Erase heading not required.)

Place	Date	Hour	Summary of Events and Information	Remarks and references to Appendices
SALEUX	8.4.18 to 11.4.18		Arrived at SALEUX about 3am - Billets were very crowded. The day was spent in cleaning up. The Brigade remained here at rest until the 11th inst. Orders were received at 4pm 10th inst to move to the 115 Brigade	
BELLOY.	12.4.18 13.4.18		marched to BELLOY when they arrived about midnight. At 9 am 12 inst the Brigade moved on to CANDAS arriving about 3 pm moved out at dawn next day (13th inst) to the aerodrome outside the village to make room for French troops. At 2pm 13 L the Brigade marched on to GEZINCOURT arriving at 5 pm. No billets were available the batteries camped out until	
	14.4.18		time to move on to DOULLENS. Entraining at DOULLENS began on the night 14/15 in the following order D.C.B.A. HQ. + on the 15th they detrained in the CASSEL area	
ST MARIE CAPPEL	15.4.18		The aerodrome near ST MARIE CAPPEL was taken over for billeting the Divl Artillery where they remained till midday 16th inst when urgent orders were received to go into action under orders of 25th D.A. behind the	
RENINGHELST	16.4.18		SCHERPENBERG (SHEET 28 M.18.c) + form the 49th Divn Infantry. Position were taken up in M.11.b.+ce.- HQ established at NIEWE MANN EST. new gun positions. W.L. are on the RENINGHELST - ABEELE ROAD	

149 Bde RFA
Army Form C. 2118.

WAR DIARY
or
INTELLIGENCE SUMMARY.
(Erase heading not required.)

APRIL 1918   Sheet 1/1

Place	Date	Hour	Summary of Events and Information	Remarks and references to Appendices
	17/5.		Brigade O.P. established at M.2.c.1.8 + batteries registered - O.P.s were manned nightly day. The brigade was held in reserve. The CRA visited batteries on the 18th.	
	19/5.		French (84 Div) took over the line in front of us & several 77 batteries took up positions in this area. Assisted the French Artillery in concentration shoots & night harassing fire. The firing done in the day time.	
	20-22/5.			
	22.		The Brigade withdrew to W.L. after dusk - all clear by 7 p.m. + came under orders of the CRA 49 Div. Enemy attacked the French that evening but gained little ground.	
	23.		Reconnoitred positions around SWAN CHATEAU (I.19) under 49 DA (22 Corps) opened up at dusk. HQ established in H.21.b.2.2. A/Bty in position at IRON BRIDGE (I.26.c) B.C.D in I.19.a + H.24.b. HQ + D Major L was were called efrient to wreconute - taking up L in room 300x away.	
	24.		O.P. established on H.1.b.60. Major L was again shelled out during the night 24/25 aspect the night on the work	
	25.		New W.L were reconnoited for the brigade occupied in area of H.16.a + H.17.c	

149 Bde R.F.A.

Army Form C. 2118.

APRIL 1918 Sheet IV

WAR DIARY
or
INTELLIGENCE SUMMARY.
(Erase heading not required.)

Instructions regarding War Diaries and Intelligence Summaries are contained in F. S. Regs., Part II. and the Staff Manual respectively. Title pages will be prepared in manuscript.

Place	Date	Hour	Summary of Events and Information	Remarks and references to Appendices
H.21.b.2.2.	25/4/18	3.00am	Enemy very heavily shelled our back area with some gas shelling also from the S.E. & attacked the line in front of KEMMEL-SHERPENBERG-WYTSCHAETE. The attack was made on our front but our battery positions were affected with the shelling & some men in D/149 were gassed. Enemy captured KEMMEL HILL & La CLYTTE. This necessitated the withdrawal of our forward battery (A) which after dark withdrew to position in H.16.c	
	26/4/18		The day opened very quietly but at 9.15am the enemy re-opened the attack under cover of the mist. After very heavy fighting which lasted till 11am the enemy succeeded in pushing back our line on to the following:– N. & central – S. of VOORMEZEELE – LOCK 7 – LOCK 8 – LA CHAPELLE – N. of BLUFF. In the evening B. & D batteries withdrew to positions in H.15.a.& b. The line on our left on the OTRLING CASTLE – HILL 60 ridge was given up during the night. The brigade now covered the 110 T Brigade.	
	27/4/18		Enemy quiet except during night – Our artillery carried out harassing fire & fired counter preparations in the early morning.	

149 Bde RFA

Army Form C. 2118.

WAR DIARY
or
INTELLIGENCE SUMMARY.

APRIL 1918   Sheet V

Place	Date	Hour	Summary of Events and Information	Remarks and references to Appendices
H.21.c.2.3.	28/4/18		Quieter day - Enemy shelled A/Bty position, causing a few casualties, during the night 28/29. A Prisoner captured near VOORMEZEELE warned us that the enemy intended to make further attack on YPRES on the following day - every precaution was taken but no attack developed.	
	29/4/18		Orders received to take over the line from 51 Bde RFA on one night - but same were afterwards cancelled. Enemy further attempted to force positions on our right but were unsuccessful. A concentration of the enemy round VOORMEZEELE was spotted by one F.O.O. + completely dispersed by our guns. Harassing fire carried out during the night.	
	30/4/18		Quiet day - very little shelling by the enemy who was reported to be moving up his guns. Two or three very overnight shoots on enemy movement were carried out. Two T.M. batteries were effectively silenced by our Howr Battery.	

3/5/18.

R. H. Pearson 2/Lt. R the I.O.
Dr O/C 149 Bde R.F.A.

149 Bde RFA
Army Form C. 2118.

WAR DIARY
or
INTELLIGENCE SUMMARY.
(Erase heading not required.)

APRIL 1918   Sheet V1

Place	Date	Hour	Summary of Events and Information	Remarks and references to Appendices
Appendices				
	2nd to end		During the month the following Officers joined the Brigade.	
			Capt A.G. Parsons joined C Battery	
			2/Lt E.T Burton attached to A Battery	
			Lieut P. Heenan attached to D Battery.	
			The following Officers were struck off the strength during the month for the following reasons as stated	
	26 Ind		Capt A.G Parsons C/149 Killed in action.	
	21 st		H.Hon Major Thellusson attached to 148 Brigade as C.O.	
			Cpt Henry Gunderson posted to 149 R.D.A. as Staff Officer	
	29		Major In Macfarlane attached to 1st Army H.Q	
	19		Lieut J.D Bell B/149. To England Sick	
	9		Major A Nickous to R.A 111 Corps.	
	30		The following casualties were received. 4/4/18. 46. O.R. + 22/4/18. 21. O.R.	
			There were 3. O.R. Killed, and 9. O.R. wounded during the month	

149 Bde RFA
Army Form C. 2118.
APRIL 1918 Sheet VII

WAR DIARY
INTELLIGENCE SUMMARY.

Place	Date	Hour	Summary of Events and Information	Remarks and references to Appendices
Appendices				
	11		The undermentioned Officers & men were "mentioned" during the month for gallantry in action	
			Lieut B. Howell. received the Military Cross	
			Act of gallantry	
			3 uby o R.d.M. E P Faulkner A/149	
			10082 Sgt R Dooley A/149	
			10173 Bdr H Smith. C/149	
			97949 Gnr E Chatwin C/149	
			219436 Gnr W Smart B/149	
			705213 " C Johnson	
			237191. C Robinson	
			4/900 G Withington	
			219690 2/Bom J Frost	
			19628 Sgt A Chandley	
			10440 Gnr R Buckley MM C/149	
			...A/Cpl. C/149	

SECRET.

WAR DIARY.

149TH. BRIGADE R.F.A.

MAY 1918.

VOLUME 31.

WAR DIARY
INTELLIGENCE SUMMARY

Army Form C. 2118.

MAY 1918

Place	Date	Hour	Summary of Events and Information	Remarks and references to Appendices
Maps	5/5/18		In action N. of YPRES covering front from S.O. ZILLEBEKE LAKE to LOCK 8 on CANAL	
	8/5/18		Moved to cover RIDGE road to VOORMEZEELE front, changing position with 211th Bde RFA (4g Dn)	
			French position in neighbourhood of LOCRE 4 am. Barrage put down to assist (49 Dn.)	
			Enemy attack of bombardment beginning 1 am. Guns shelled & calibre, to very partion heavily	
			Gas shells 3 am - 2pm afternoon Enemy attacked LA CLYTTE - VOORMEZEELE front	
			Got firmstop scrooms late. Bde relieved by 156 Bde RFA of the day trough attack.	
			After marched to STAPLE arr. during morning (20 miles)	
	9/5/18		In action again relieving 64 Bde RFA in front METEREN. A/Bde and W. adjoining French	
	10/5/18		All quiet.	
	11/5/18		Barrage shells & morning. Some casualties.	
			10-3 1/2 hrs between 3am + 5am.	
			HQ moved.	
	17/5/18		BCD batteries Shelled. Some casualties. 3 guns per battery moved to new positions	
	18/5/18		C Bty. heavily shelled.	
	19-20/5/18		Good deal of enemy shelling changing fire on both sides, heaviest during night	
	31/5/18		Bde. relieved by 59th Bde RFA (11 D.A.) Withdraw for rest & training in RECQUINGHEM area, S. of SAMER.	
			2 Platis, Adjt, A/Bde P/6, RTO 1/8/5.	

SECRET
91/32

War Diary
149th Brigade R.F.A.
July 1918.

Vol.

WAR DIARY
or
INTELLIGENCE SUMMARY.
(Erase heading not required.)

Army Form C. 2118.

Place	Date	Hour	Summary of Events and Information	Remarks and references to Appendices
Field	1st July		Brigade carried out action to wagon lines in EECUS area (NB A/lug July 31st Army School)	
	2nd		Brigade marched to TEENVOORDE Area (TERDEGHEM). Reconnoitred positions to take over from French behind front in Cat.	
	4th		Brigade in position (in reserve) covering reconstructed Wing 71st French Division (reinforced Cta)	
	8th		Brigade with 35 Div. taken over from French.	
	10th		Disarmament inspection by Army Commander	
	12th		Bde HQ + 2 actions for battery withdrawn to Wagon lines, to go in wet training	
	13-15		New positions reconnoitred for defense of "Army line" & Bty. changed position (twice)	
	18th		Moves to new positions carried on. Extensive Aero training at Wagon line. Actions open as lot of two yon. Whiles in competition	
	24th		Inspection (armed of Wipth mounted Parade) by × Corps Commander ⟨Eqc 30 Dimon⟩	
	26th		Reconnoitred field position in support of return as left of 35th Div	
	27th		Reconnoitred field position forward began in turn	
	31st		Bde went into action to support 35 Div. with positions eventually prepared by 77 Bde RFA.	

R. Davidson Col RFA
COLONEL
COMDG 158TH COUNTY DURHAM

WR 33

SECRET.

149th BRIGADE (COUNTY PALATINE) ROYAL FIELD ARTILLERY.

WAR DIARY.

AUGUST 1918.

Army Form C. 2118.

WAR DIARY
or
INTELLIGENCE SUMMARY.
(Erase heading not required.)

Instructions regarding War Diaries and Intelligence Summaries are contained in F.S. Regs., Part II. and the Staff Manual respectively. Title pages will be prepared in manuscript.

Place	Date	Hour	Summary of Events and Information	Remarks and references to Appendices
R 11	11/8/18		Division relieved in Corps Reserve, 1 section per Bn in return	
Sect 29	11/8/16		about R.1 & over Button & Second Line.	
R 6	12/8/16		Brigade relieving 159th Bde R.F.A. covering the Loos salient junction	
			H.Q. Rgs. ABY in M.13 B.89m M.12 d.4. 835m M.7 D.6" m M.184	
			Relief in the positions forward positions was sheep + all batteries	
			were in communication in the attack on the enemy wired accepted	
			successfully in capturing the Dummentz Ridge & gun lines 2.5 am	
21/8/16			on the 21 inst. This mi resulting in the enemy counter	
31/8/16			our guns gunwell and on the 31st enemy Renewed ful.	
	5/9/18			

Robertson Lt./Adjt.
109 Bdf. F.A.

SECRET.

30th (BRITISH) DIVISION.

WAR DIARY.

149th BRIGADE R.F.A.

SEPTEMBER 1918.

Army Form C. 2118.

WAR DIARY
or
INTELLIGENCE SUMMARY.
(Erase heading not required.)

Instructions regarding War Diaries and Intelligence
Summaries are contained in F. S. Regs., Part II.
and the Staff Manual respectively. Title pages
will be prepared in manuscript.

Place	Date	Hour	Summary of Events and Information	Remarks and references to Appendices
	1918			
	1st Sept		Headquarters moved into the area of Lierre Château. Batteries into Drummin Reus	
	3rd "		" " up the road of Drummin	
	10th "		" " St. MEUVE EGLISE Tilot	
	24th "		Formed a desert hut in their dugout. D but T but 2 officers 2nd Lt 2nd Lt Anderson killed 2nd Lieut	
			2nd Lt Parker wounded	
	25th		Brigade got down a Sunday leaving. Two and R. Infantry Brigade apart went forward during the afternoon. At our C Bat lost 1 Officer 2nd Lieut J. B. Dunlop wounded	
	28th		Brigade moved at 9 am. Two new positions near WULVERGHEM. R. Destroyed gun in readiness for R. Bullet. Result of which MESSINES & WYTSCHAETE being taken. Heather Quantity M.C. cells being ammoned with good results	
	During		On arrival Brigade arrival met a heavy programme of turning over and many enemy T.M. shoots were carried out as also M.C. cells replied to	
	Month		Brigade ammoved at trying in from West to East from L.10 to L.30. a distance of	
			5000 yards	
				E.W. Hunt Lieut
				for J. Pt. 14 O. R.A.
				R.F.A.

Vol 35

SECRET.

30th (BRITISH) DIVISION.

WAR DIARY.

149th BRIGADE R.F.A.

OCTOBER 1918.

WAR DIARY or INTELLIGENCE SUMMARY

Army Form C. 2118.

Place	Date	Hour	Summary of Events and Information	Remarks and references to Appendices
	1/10/18		Brigade moved forward to TENBRIELEN AREA Sheet 28 P.16 & 17	
	3/10/18		on account of battle for our Fr positions Pg. 10 & 13 - H.Q. moved to P.3.d	
	14/10/18		30th Division having taken all objectives N of WERVICQ Brigade wasn ordered into AREA GHELUWE	
	15/10/18		Batteries moved up to positions allotted about 28 Q.9.2.3	
	16/10/18		H.Q. moved to Q.9.2.3.	
	18/10/18		Brigade moved forward to cross the 9th & 2nd Inf. Bde marching at 06.00 and crossed the pontoon bridges over R.LYS Brookseyne by 09.30 & near the trough RONCQ and DRONKAARD halting at CROISE where B & C batteries got into action being on special targets "B" hall by machine gun fire though firing during the afternoon I.E.A.	
	19/10/18		Brigade again moved forward to STERHOEK abt 30.5.5.a Bdy Hdrs who action in M.35.a and S.18.a T.13.a	
	20/10/18		Infantry having occurred the attack gaining the objectives Brigade followed up through ZEVECOTEN to PETIT TOURCOING battery going into action in T.15 & T.16.c	

WAR DIARY
or
INTELLIGENCE SUMMARY

Army Form C. 2118.

Place	Date	Hour	Summary of Events and Information	Remarks and references to Appendices
	21/10/18		The 90th Infantry Brigade having gained their final objective on the D.L. Decent were relieved by the 80th Infantry Brigade. 38th H.F.A. relieved the 140th Bde. The batteries pulling out to their Wagon Lines	
	23/10/18		By a long shell shell "B" battery lost 3 men killed & wounded 17 horses killed. 13 wounded	
	24/10/18		"D" battery went into action for a special shoot to assist the 34 Div pulling out as soon as over.	
	30/10/18		"D" battery again into action relieving after the shoot to their W lines to await day.	
			BRIGADE covered during the month in the advance 38500X onglongs as a direct line WEST to EAST of 34300 x 5.	

1/11/18

[signature]
for C.O.
140th Brigade R.F.A.

WARDIA

SECRET.

30th (BRITISH) DIVISION.

WAR DIARY.

NOVEMBER 1918.

149th BRIGADE R.F.A.

WAR DIARY
INTELLIGENCE SUMMARY.
(Erase heading not required.)

Army Form C. 2118.

Place	Date	Hour	Summary of Events and Information	Remarks and references to Appendices
HEESTERT.	1/11/18		The Brigade reconnoitred positions to take over from 41st Division.	
"	2/11/18		Brigade moved up into relieve covering 90th I.B. (opening) Brigade HQ being in area of HEESTERT.	
"	4/11/18 to 8/11/18		No change in situation, slight shelling & battery positions, 1 casualty reported.	
"	9/11/18		Enemy evacuating E bank of L'ESCAUT River. Brigade reconnoitred 1 section, not following up the enemy.	
"	10/11/18		Unopposed recces. 1 ammoniac received 22.30 hrs.	
"	11/11/18		Wire received from Front H.Q. to G.9777 to the effect that hostilities will cease at 11.00 hrs Nov 11".	
"	12/11/18		Bulletins posting to RENAIX AREA.	
"	15/11/18		Under orders rcvd Brigade moved back to ST ANNE & AELBEKE AREA	
"	K 30/11/18		Bde reconnoitred at AELBEKE.	

[signatures]

J.O.C., 145 Bde R.F.A.

Vol 37

SECRET.

W A R   D I A R Y

149th BRIGADE, R.F.A. 30th DIVISION.

1/31st DECEMBER, 1918.

WAR DIARY
or
INTELLIGENCE SUMMARY.
(Erase heading not required.)

Army Form C. 2118.

Place	Date	Hour	Summary of Events and Information	Remarks and references to Appendices
AELBEKE	2/12/18		Left for AIRE and arrived in area East of ARMENTIERES.	
	3/12/18		Brigade continued march to AIRE and on arrival occupied "B" Barracks.	
	4/12/18 to 31/12/18		In Barracks at AIRE	

[signature]
Captain R.F.A.
Adjutant, 149th Brigade R.F.A.

CONFIDENTIAL

WAR DIARY

of

149th BRIGADE, R.F.A.

FROM: 1st January, 1919 to 31st January, 1919.

WAR DIARY
or
INTELLIGENCE SUMMARY
(Erase heading not required.)

Army Form C. 2118.

Place	Date	Hour	Summary of Events and Information	Remarks and references to Appendices
AIRE	1/1/19 to 31/1/19		In "B" Barracks for Demobilization	

A. Harris Lieut. R.F.A.
of Adjutant, 149th Brigade, R.F.A.

Army Form C. 2118.

Vol 39

WAR DIARY
or
INTELLIGENCE SUMMARY.
(Erase heading not required.)

Place	Date	Hour	Summary of Events and Information	Remarks and references to Appendices
AIRE	1/2/19 to 29/2/19		At 'A' Barracks for demobilization	

A Menzies Captain RFA
for O.C 149th Brigade RFA

Army Form C. 2118.

WAR DIARY

~~INTELLIGENCE SUMMARY~~

(Erase heading not required.)

149 Bde R.F.A.

Vol 41

Instructions regarding War Diaries and Intelligence Summaries are contained in F. S. Regs., Part II. and the Staff Manual respectively. Title pages will be prepared in manuscript.

Place	Date	Hour	Summary of Events and Information	Remarks and references to Appendices
	1-4-19 to 30-4-19		Brigade located at "B" Barracks, AIRE.	
			Demobilization of personnel and disposal of horses proceeded with.	
	30-4-19		Strength 30-4-19:- Officers 10. O.R's 257. Animals 16 mules.	

[signature]

Capt. R.F.A.

for O.C. 149th. Brigade R.F.A.